Butterfly Express

by Jane Belk Moncure
illustrated by Linda Hohag

Published by  **THE CHILD'S WORLD**®

Mankato, Minnesota

 **GROLIER**

Your partner in education

Distributed by Grolier, Sherman Turnpike
Danbury, Connecticut 06816

The Library —
A Magic Castle

Come to the magic castle
When you are growing tall.
Rows upon rows of Word Windows
Line every single wall.
They reach up high,
As high as the sky,
And you want to open them all.
For every time you open one,
A new adventure has begun.

Nicole opened
a Word Window.
Here is what she read.

A little girl found a caterpillar in a field one day. It was all alone. "Hi," said the little girl.

She put her hand down near
the caterpillar. It climbed up
one finger and down another.

"I will take you home with me,"
said the little girl. And she did.

8

Her father made a cage for the
caterpillar out of two pie pans
and some screen wire.

The little girl put leaves and a
stick in the cage.

She put the cage in a sunny
window and there it stayed.

Every day the caterpillar ate leaves,
and every day it grew bigger.

One day it wiggled out of its skin.
Its new skin fit just right.

Each time the caterpillar wiggled
out of its old skin, it was bigger.

Then one day it climbed up on the stick and made a tiny button of silk.

The caterpillar hung upside down from the silk and . . .

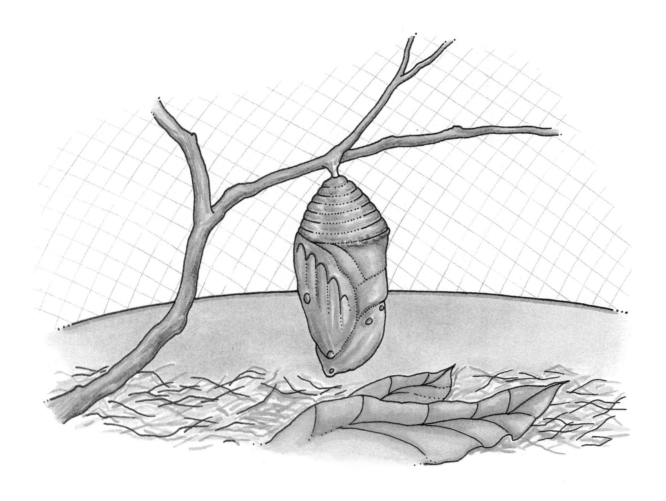

wiggled out of its skin for the last time. But this time, there was a green shell underneath the old skin.

"When your caterpillar comes out of its shell, it will not be a caterpillar at all," said the girl's mother.

"What will it be?" asked the girl.

"It will be a surprise," said her
mother. "Wait and see."

So the little girl waited . . .

and looked for the surprise.

The little girl wished she could see
what was happening inside the
shell. But she could not.

Still she waited and watched.

Finally, one day, she peeked in
the cage and saw . . .

a beautiful butterfly! What a surprise!

So that was what had been happening inside the shell. The caterpillar was changing into a butterfly.

"How pretty," said the little girl. Then she looked outside and saw another surprise. Snow!

"This could be trouble," said her
father. "The early snow is covering
the flowers.

The butterfly must drink nectar from the flowers or it will die."

"What can we do?" asked the little girl.

"I know where flowers grow in the wintertime," said her father. "In California."

Guess what he did?

He called a friend who was an airplane pilot.

"Yes," said the pilot. "I am flying to California today. I will take the butterfly with me."

The little girl put her butterfly
in a box with holes in the top.
She wrote . . .

The pilot took the butterfly with him all the way to California.

There he opened the box. Away
flew the butterfly . . .